P9-BHT-939

Variety of Life

Insects

Please visit our web site at: www.garethstevens.com
For a free color catalog describing Gareth Stevens Publishing's
list of high-quality books and multimedia programs, call
1-800-542-2595 (USA) or 1-800-387-3178 (Canada).
Gareth Stevens Publishing's fax: (414) 332-3567.

Library of Congress Cataloging-in-Publication Data

Richardson, Joy.
    Insects / Joy Richardson. — North American ed.
        p. cm. — (Variety of life)
    Includes bibliographical references and index.
    ISBN 0-8368-4505-6 (lib. bdg.)
        1. Insects—Juvenile literature. I. Title.
    QL467.2.R534   2005
    595.7—dc22   2004058987

This North American edition first published in 2005 by
Gareth Stevens Publishing
A WRC Media Company
330 West Olive Street, Suite 100
Milwaukee, Wisconsin 53212 USA

This U.S. edition copyright © 2005 by Gareth Stevens, Inc.
Original editions copyright © 1993 and 2003 by Franklin Watts.
First published in 1993 by Franklin Watts, 96 Leonard Street,
London EC2A 4XD, England.

Franklin Watts Editors: Sarah Ridley and Sally Luck
Franklin Watts Designer: Janet Watson
Picture Research: Sarah Moule

Gareth Stevens Editor: Dorothy L. Gibbs
Gareth Stevens Designer: Kami Koenig

Picture credits: Bruce Coleman, Ltd. – 7, 9, 15, 17, 21; Robert Harding
Picture Library – 19; Frank Lane Picture Agency – 13; Natural History
Photographic Agency – cover, 3, 11, 23, 25, 27.

All rights reserved. No part of this book may be reproduced, stored in
a retrieval system, or transmitted in any form or by any means, electronic,
mechanical, photocopying, recording, or otherwise, without the prior
written permission of the copyright holder.

Printed in the United States of America

1 2 3 4 5 6 7 8 9 09 08 07 06 05

Variety of Life

Joy Richardson

Insects

GARETH**STEVENS**
PUBLISHING
A WRC Media Company

Contents

Words that appear in the glossary are printed in **boldface** type the first time they occur in the text.

Insects Everywhere

The world is full of insects.

For each person in the world, there are about one hundred million insects, and there are hundreds of thousands of different types of insects.

The world needs insects. Although some insects do a lot of damage, most insects do a lot of good, too.

Lots of ladybugs are good for a garden. They eat other insects that damage plants.

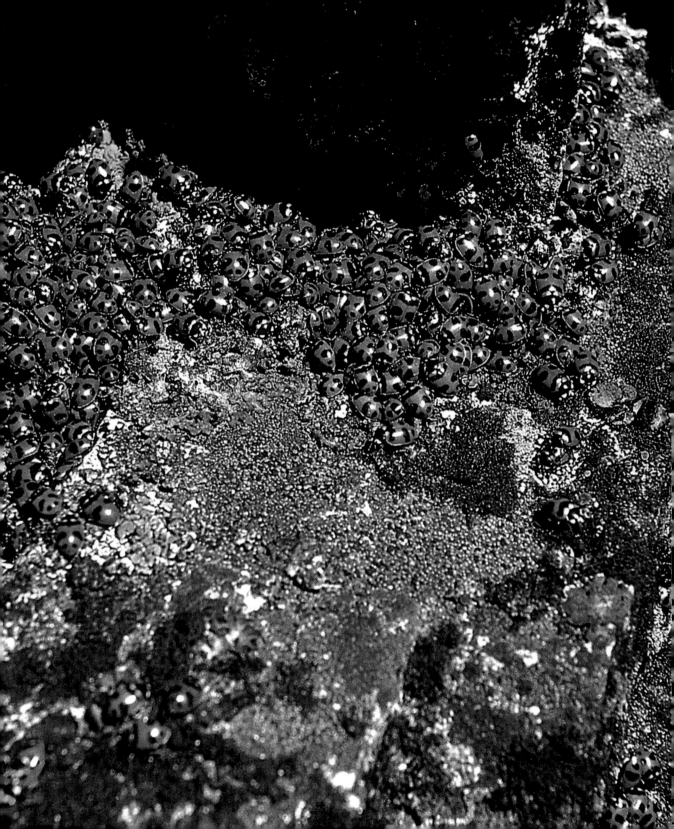

Laying Eggs

Every insect starts life inside an egg.

Female insects lay eggs. The eggs usually come out of a female insect's body through a tube at the tip of the insect's **abdomen**.

A female insect lays her eggs near food so the young insects will have something to eat after they **hatch**.

Some insects **drill** into leaves or seeds to lay their eggs. Others lay their eggs in holes underground. Some eggs are glued to leaves, wood, or rocks with a sticky liquid that female insects make inside their bodies.

This butterfly is laying eggs and gluing them to the underside of a leaf.

Starting Life

A newborn insect is called a **larva**. When there is more than one larva, they are called **larvae**.

Most insect larvae do not look like their parents.

When the egg of a butterfly hatches, a caterpillar crawls out. The caterpillar eats lots of plants. As it grows longer and fatter, it **sheds** its skin — several times!

When the caterpillar is fully grown, it prepares for a big change.

These caterpillars look very different from the butterflies they will soon become.

Time for a Change

A caterpillar that is ready to become a butterfly stops eating and gets to work.

First, it attaches itself to a plant. Then, it spins a kind of **cocoon**, called a chrysalis, around its body. The caterpillar is now a **pupa**.

The pupa rests quietly inside its protective **casing** while its whole body changes, and its legs and **wings** start to grow. Sometimes, these changes take only a few days, and sometimes, they take more than a year.

When a caterpillar has finished changing into a butterfly, it breaks out of its chrysalis.

This monarch butterfly has just come out of its chrysalis. ➡

Growing Up

Different insects grow up in different ways.

Bees and wasps build **nests**, where their larvae live safely until they change into adults.

Stick insects, or walkingsticks, hatch from their eggs looking like **miniature** adults. As they grow bigger, they shed old, **outgrown** skin and replace it with new skin.

Caddis fly larvae live underwater. They make nests out of sand, stones, leaves, and plant stems to hide in while they grow their wings.

A caddis fly larva is coming out of its underwater nest of stems and stones.

Tough Skin

Insects do not have bones. The **skeleton** of an insect is on the outside of its body.

An insect's skeleton is a hard casing, or shell, of tough skin called the **cuticle**. All the **muscles** that move the insect's legs and wings are attached to the inside of the cuticle.

The cuticle protects the insect's soft insides and helps keep them from drying out.

A male stag beetle's tough cuticle is like a suit of armor. This hard shell helps keep other animals from eating the beetle.

A Three-Part Body

The body of an adult insect has three main parts.

1) The head is at the front of the body.

2) The **thorax** is in the middle of the body. The insect's legs and wings are attached to the thorax.

3) The abdomen is at the back of the body. It is usually the biggest part of the body.

These parts are made up of **segments**, which make them able to bend.

This photograph of a wasp clearly shows its head, thorax, and large abdomen. ➡

Breathing

Insects do not breathe through noses or mouths. They breathe through airholes along the sides of their bodies.

An insect's airholes are called **spiracles**. Tubes from the spiracles **branch out** to every part of the insect's body.

Oxygen from the air that comes in through the spiracles passes into the insect's muscles to make energy. Lots of air goes to the thorax, where lots of energy is needed for moving the legs and wings.

The nine black spots on the side of this caterpillar are spiracles. The caterpillar has nine more of these airholes on the other side of its body. ➡

Legs

All insects have six legs. All of the legs are attached to the thorax.

The legs have **joints** so they can bend.

Insects are **steady** walkers. They always keep a triangle of three legs on the ground while they move the other three legs.

The ends of insects' legs have tiny claws and sticky pads, which make insects able to walk upside down.

Crane flies use the claws and sticky pads at the ends of their legs to help them hang from plants.

Wings

Most insects can fly. They have one or two pairs of wings attached to the thorax. Muscles make the wings move.

Some flies can **beat** their wings hundreds of times in one second.

Beetles hide their wings. Their front wings look like the shells that cover their bodies. When a beetle flies, it lifts its front wings, and its back wings unfold.

Dragonflies keep their two pairs of wings spread while they **glide** and **swoop** down on smaller insects.

Emperor dragonflies have huge wings and can fly very quickly.

Heads

The head of an insect has two large eyes and two **antennae**.

An insect's eyes are on the sides of its head, which means that it can see all around it. Insects cannot see very clearly, but they can spot even the smallest movements.

An insect's antennae are on the front of its head. Their antennae give insects information about touch, tastes, sounds, and smells.

A moth's large eyes are made up of thousands of smaller eyes. Moths use their antennae mainly to smell.

Insect Facts

There are all different kinds of insects in the world, but they are the same in many ways.

- All insects lay eggs.

- The bodies of all insects have three main parts and a skeleton on the outside.

- All insects have airholes along their sides and six legs attached to a thorax.

- All insects have large eyes and antennae on their heads.

Not all creepy crawly creatures are insects. Although they may have a lot in common with insects, spiders, centipedes, wood lice, and worms are not insects.

For More Facts . . .

Books

Beetles and Other Bugs. Awesome Bugs (series).
  Anna Claybourne (Copper Beech Books)

*How Do Flies Walk Upside Down? Questions and Answers
  about Insects.* Melvin and Gilda Berger (Scholastic)

Insects Grow and Change. How & Why? (series).
  Elaine Pascoe (Gareth Stevens)

Investigating Insects with a Scientist. I Like Science! (series).
  Patricia J. Murphy (Enslow)

Web Sites

Amazing Insects
  www.ivyhall.district96.k12.il.us/4th/kkhp/1insects/buginfo.html

BrainPOP Diversity of Life: Insects
  www.brainpop.com/science/diversityoflife/insects/

Katerpillars (& Mystery Bugs)
  www.uky.edu/agriculture/entomology/ythfacts/entyouth.htm

Glossary

abdomen: the largest part of an insect's body; the back or end part of an insect's body

antennae: (sometimes called "feelers") long, thin body parts on the front of an insect's head, which help the insect feel, taste, hear, and smell

beat: (v) to move up and down, hitting the air with great force

branch out: to spread like the branches of a tree

casing: a small, boxlike enclosure made out of a hard or strong material

cocoon: the silky casing that protects an insect while it is a pupa. A butterfly's cocoon is called a chrysalis.

cuticle: the tough outer layer of skin that forms the shell, or skeleton, of an insect

drill: (v) to make a hole as if using a drilling tool

glide: to float on moving air

hatch: to break out of an egg

joints: the places where two parts of something meet or join and can usually bend. In humans, bones meet at joints such as the knee or elbow.

larva (larvae): the wormlike form of many insects when they first hatch

miniature: having the same appearance but a much smaller size than is normal for a particular animal or object

muscles: the strong, stretchy tissues that make bones and other body parts able to move

nests: the shelters made by animals such as birds and insects to hold their eggs and protect their young

outgrown: no longer large enough to hold whatever is kept or is growing inside

oxygen: a colorless, odorless, tasteless gas that all animals need to breathe to stay alive

pupa (pupae): the form of an insect while it is changing from a larva into an adult

segments: small sections or divisions of a single object

sheds: (v) drops or lets fall off

skeleton: a shape made of bones, or some other bony or hard material, that forms the body of an animal

spiracles: breathing holes; small openings through which air enters for breathing

steady: well-balanced; not wobbly or likely to slip or fall

swoop: to make a quick, smooth, downward movement while flying

thorax: the middle part of an insect's body, to which the legs and wings are attached

wings: the parts of a bird's or an insect's body that are used for flying. Insects have one or two pairs of wings.

Index